# Special
# Tour

Sophia Jones

Inquiries and Book Orders should be addressed to:

 Great Writers Media

Great Writers Media
Email: info@greatwritersmedia.com
Phone: 877-600-5469

ISBN: 978-1-960939-17-3 (sc)
ISBN: 978-1-960939-18-0 (ebk)

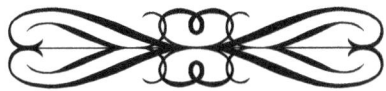

It was around Thanksgiving when I arrived in this world. Earlier the year I was born my parents experienced the loss of my older sister. They were heart broken, she was not quite a year old when she died. As a result of the loss of a child my parents grief caused them to be protective of their other children When I arrived in this world they felt the joy and the chance to love the child they were blessed with.

When I was a little older and ready for solid foods the trend was to feed children from the food served to the family. My mom would normally have mashed some potatoes and put gravy on them to feed me. My mother refused to take the chance of feeding me the old fashioned way, she feared I might choke. There were products on the market designed to feed the latest addition to any family. My parents decided to buy jars of baby food for the very first time. A small child eating adult foods was considered to be dangerous. Babies needed to have a few teeth and learn to chew the foods. My mother wanted to be sure I was not going to choke on food. She was determined to make certain I would grow up.

When I was a little older I heard my older sister and brother tell their friends they call me special. I thought it was my name and did not understand why they called me special when my parents called me a different name. I was confused and thought I had two names.

Now that I am older and have gone through a series of health issue I know just how special I am. Feeling bad when I hear my siblings or someone else talking about me being treated special doesn't hurt anymore.

I am able to walk so I explore the area where I live with my family. We live in a rural area with a few neighbors in walking distance. I am not allowed to go outside alone as the road is close to the yard. My parents are always reliving the fear of losing another child, I guess it is hard to overcome fears. I usually have an older brother or sister with me. On the rare occasions when I am allowed to go outside alone I may not leave the concrete back porch.

From the porch I can see the into the kitchen or the area that is our yard and garden. We live in a fairly big house, with a large kitchen and living room. The dining room is small and there is a spare bedroom downstairs for guests. My mother spends a lot of time in the kitchen preparing meals and preserving foods for the winter.

My father who is a jack of all trades recently painted the walls and ceiling and put new tile on the kitchen floor. I think we may have just moved into the house. There is a combination coal/gas stove for cooking and heating the kitchen. We do not have central heat in the house yet. The refrigerator is small compared to the refrigerators of today, but it served the purpose. There is a sink and my dad did the plumbing so we had running water till the hand dug well went dry. The kitchen table where we eat our meals is large with blue wooden legs I still crawl around under the table sometimes. There are chairs for the adults and a green bench along the wall for the smaller children to sit at meal time.

My dad had his favorite place to sit to read the mail and newspaper in the kitchen. Sometimes he holds me and reads the newspaper to me. I do not understand what he reads to me. My dad is just keeping me out of the way as my mother prepares meals so I do not get burned. I know I was extremely sheltered from danger as a child.

When I looked out the window behind my dads favorite chair I can see a sloped roof.

When I stand looking out the kitchen door I could see the porch with the roof being held up by fancy red brick pillars. I can see the pig pen and the out house at the edge of the porch. The out buildings are painted barn red with an odor all their own so we don't open the screen door on hot summer days. We did not have a flushing toilet inside the house like the modern homes have.

My dad laid the bricks for the pillars they had a white concrete block three feet up from the porch. The rest of the way to the roof the brick pillars were smaller in width. My father was a brick layer before he took a better paying job.

He works a swing shift on his new job, sometimes 7-3, or 3-11 and sometimes 11-7 in the morning. When he would leave for work after lunch he would give my mother a kiss and then rub his face on my face and tell me to be a good girl. His whiskers were rough on the tender skin of my face.

I want to go along with my dad to work sometimes and scream and have a temper tantrum when I don't get my own way. That usually get me a nap as I would not be cranky if I was not tired.

My mother works days during the Summer months when school is out and the older family members can babysit. She works in the clothing manufacturing industry evenings during the school year.

My older sister is babysitting today as both my parents are working. I get to go outside today. I walk along the side of the porch I see some steps. I follow them and it takes me to a smaller concrete landing and the entrance to the outside basement steps. The steps are attached to the foundation of the house.

The roof over the cellar steps was covered with tin from the garage.

I get older and our parents are both working the day shift. It is the summer so my older siblings baby sit for us. They take waxed paper from the kitchen and sit on it to slide down the tin roof. These are the things we do to amuse ourselves sometimes we play hide and seek, tag or red light green light. My parents don't want us using the roof as a sliding board. I guess when they remember the things they did as children they are afraid for us. We could would fall off the higher side of the roof and break bones. I can see into the kitchen when I am on the tin roof.

I go outside to play mostly when my older brothers and sisters are babysitting.

Then the next day that I am outside I take a walk to the other side of the porch. I take one step down and I am on the long sidewalk. I walked the length of the sidewalk and am very close to the road, mailbox and the tin garage. When I got to the mailbox I could see a large field across the street. It did not take long before my sister came looking for me. On the left side of the walk was our garden, we had two goose berry bushes, a currant berry bush and some rhubarb planted there.

It was time to plant the garden before school ended for the summer. The boys and my dad turned the soil for the garden. The garden is larger than our kitchen.

I looked farther to my left past the garden and see a big dirt pile. On the other side of the dirt pile I can see the roof top of a house. I am able to see the whole house from the top of the pile. I am no longer in our yard so I need to go back to the porch to play or some one will come looking for me.

Today my younger sister and I are allowed to play outside again. It is time to plant the garden again, so the entire family is outside working in the garden planting seeds. I see them plant beans, corn, lettuce, peas and red beet seeds. They will plant tomato plants, pepper plants and cabbage after we have had the last frost of the season. It must be a Saturday no one is in school and my parents are off from work. My sister and I are playing on the dirt pile digging in the ground to make mud pies.

Everyone is called in the house for lunch we are called to wash up. We didn't need to take a nap after lunch today so it was back outside to work in the garden. We are allowed to play while everyone else worked at planting the garden finished. We always have to wash up for meals, even if we are not dirty from playing outside. Today after all the gardening work everyone was tired so no bath was given to my sister and I. We did not care we were tired and were already falling asleep at the dinner table.

Walking outside again the next chance I got I followed the sidewalk to the road and looked to my left there stood the tin garage where my dad parks his car.

Directly in front of me was an ugly rickety picket fence that was falling down. It was a mustard brownish color, the road was on the other side of the fence. By the fence there is a white rose bush and another flower plant I could not identify.

Turning around to look at the house I see the front porch has 3 red brick pillars holding up the roof. There was another entrance to the house in the middle of the porch. There were two windows on the left side of the door and a single window on the right side of the door. There are three green wooden rocking chairs sitting on the front porch. There are many summer nights we sit outside playing games like hide and seek or tag even catching lightning bugs. There is a pine tree, a pear tree and a lilac bush in the yard too.

From the front yard I can see our neighbors barn and chicken coop. To get to their barn I need to cross a narrow drainage ditch. I am always to play where I can be seen. Along the one side of the ditch there are planks used to keep the ground from caving in.

The neighbors barn was in bad shape and looked like it might fall down. They no longer have farm animals since the people are very old. The oldest woman I am told is 90 and is blind. There is another woman living there, probably her daughter. She takes care of the elderly woman and the older man who lives with her. The younger woman has a son about the same age as one of my brothers. She takes care of us in her home when both of my parents work day shift and the older siblings are in school. My mother started working all year recently so we have the neighbor as a temporary baby sitter when they both work days. The family next door doesnot have electric in their home they use kerosene lamps to light the house at night. My parents are paying her to babysit so she can get the electric installed in the house.

The weather is warmer so I get to go outside more often. I see a small yellow building across the street, I am told it is a one room school house. So I ask is that where my older siblings go to school. In earlier years it is possible the building may have been used as a church cause at one time there was a bell on the roof.

I know that we have other neighbors on the left side of our property. I play with their daughter sometimes.

While outside I see another house across the street and down the road. This is where a little old man lives. He has a small orchard and is a bee keeper. We always had a good supply of his processed honey and even raw honey that he sells to my mother. The orchard he own has a few plumb trees and sometimes he brings us a few ripe plumbs.

I am allowed another day of playing outside, so I invite the neighbor girl to join my sister and I. We are playing on the dirt pile when we find these green berries. We pick them and pretend we are baking pies like our mothers do on Holidays. We need something to put the berries in. I go in the house and ask my mother for something we can put the berries in. It must be a Saturday mom is home today, she gives me plastic cups. We are content picking the berries making believe we are doing cooking for our dolls. When play time is over we need to eat lunch. We had to clean up for lunch. Since we didn't get real dirty playing outside today when we are called in to eat dinner we do wash up to eat. We do not need to have a bath before bed since we were not real dirty.

The next morning when we wake up and came down stairs our parents laugh at us. Later I find out what is so funny, we had a rash on our faces arm and legs so did our neighbor's daughter. The next thing we had to do was show our dad what we were playing with the day before. The little berries were some kind of poison, we didn't know any better. The three of us had itchy skin and our eyes were almost swelled closed from the rash. We were asked if we ate any of the berries which we did not. We have to wash often and apply a lotion to dry up the rash.

Playing outside during the harvest of the some of the garden vegetables it is near the fourth of July. The whole family is out on the back porch husking the first picking of the sweet corn. We will have corn on the cob with our meal today. There are string beans and peas ready for picking. My sister and I are playing on the dirt pile making mud pies. We get water at the hand pump and no one stops us they think we are drinking the water. We are able to be seen from the porch so when I start screaming my older sister comes to check on me. I tell her something is biting me, she looks at my bottom and sees I have some bright red bites on my bottom. She empties the tub filled with corn husk and fills it with cold water and puts me in it clothes and all. The bite marks stopped hurting right away. I had ants in my pants from sitting over an ant hill. I learned real fast to watch where I sat after that.

We have a picnic on the fourth of July. The men will carry the table out of the kitchen. We will have hot dogs, hamburgers and corn on the cob. We have mom's home made potato salad, macaroni salad and baked beans. There will be watermelon for dessert. There is so much food we will probably be eating it for the next day as well!

It is a few days into early September so the older siblings are back in school. My mother has plans to do some chores. She prepared lunch and packed a lunch for our dad to take along to work, he is working the middle shift this week. My sister and I will be in the way when mom starts the chore she planned. She decides we need a nap, she lays down on the day bed with us till we fall asleep. I don't know what she plans to do while we sleep.

I am the first to wake up and I wake my sister up for someone to play with. Well she was still sleepy so she is cranky. Mom is not happy with me, so I need to take another nap. Now I am not happy, but it is better than getting a swat on my bottom.

The next day it is the same thing after lunch it is nap time. This time when I wake up before my sister I do not wake her. I learned that lesson fast. I needed to use the bathroom. My mom helped me with that then she told me to play quietly in the room. I was soon bored, so I went into the kitchen to see what my mother was doing. I stood on my tiptoes and still could not see over the kitchen table. I asked my mom what are you doing? Can I help? She thought for a few seconds then stood me on a chair. She showed me how to fill the glass jars with the peaches she prepared. I did a good job cause when my dad came home from work she showed him she had a little helper today. I am told this will be some of the food to get us through the winter.

I have asked where do my older siblings go when they do not go to school?

My mom does not understand my question so I do not get an answer. I do not have any idea what Saturday and Sunday off from school means. I am told they go to church on Sundays and back to school on Mondays. I am curious what is school and church? I start begging to go with them to school or church. I am told that when I am old enough I will go to school. So I keep begging to go to church. I can go with them to church once I can sit still for an hour. I tell her I can do that already, so when can I go to church I ask! I will be allowed to go the very next Sunday. I feel like I won a great prize.

It is Sunday and I get all cleaned up and wear a dress today. I guess my siblings really did not want me along they walk very fast. I need to run to keep up with them, I fall and skin my knees and tear my dress. No Sunday school today they took me home to get my skinned knees treated. I am not in trouble for that, they were told they should have been holding my hand and walking slower.

My pretty pink dress is what I wore to my oldest sisters wedding. I was a flower girl so was my little sister, I don't remember much about that day.

I get to go to church every Sunday now and a little old man with white hair and a white beard sings his favorite song before Sunday school starts, he sings, Jesus loves me. He (Sam) also had a part in starting a tradition in our church called harvest home Sunday. Everyone brings in a vegetable from their garden and the produce is blessed. I walk to Sunday school with my siblings rain or shine. Sometimes a neighbor picks us up and take us along so we don't get all wet. There were 4 of us crammed into the car along with the family of the driver. Some days the neighbors walked along if the weather is nice.

I have attended Sunday school now for a few weeks and have been listening to the teacher reading from the bible. I fall in love with the stories about Jesus. He is teaching the people about his father. Isabelle the teacher is reading about the healing Jesus performs on his followers.

Now I have a question, I raise my hand to ask my question. I ask if we can do all that Jesus does then why are people sick. I know my grandfather is sick from something where he has a hard time breathing. She doesn't have an answer for me, she doesn't even offer to find an answer for me. The next Sunday I ask the same question and do this week after week. I am told you are disturbing the class with your questions, stop being a pest. You may go stand in the corner till Sunday school is over. I enjoyed going to Sunday school but most Sundays I just stood in the corner cause I knew if I asked any more questions I was going to be sent there anyway. I liked the story of Jesus bringing Lazarus back from the dead. So when I asked the teacher this time why people are still getting sick she told me people were having miracles performed by Jesus. She also said the miracles do not happen anymore.

In the church there is a picture of Jesus knocking on a door, the message is knock and the door will open. I remember trying to knock on the door and it did not open for me so I was wondering what I did wrong. I asked the teacher hat I did wrong and was told I ask too many questions.

I have learned there are many things I must learn in my life and answers are for me to find most of the time. I love to take walks outside and look at the pets we have and learn that these pets are well taken care of.

I am finally old enough for school, before I start school I need a vaccination. My parents take my sister and I along the next time they go into town. We go with our mother while our dad goes in a store. We go to this white building and sit and wait till we are invited into the next room. The nurse weighs us and then a man comes and we enter another room. There the man tells us he is going to scratch us with this thing and promises it will not hurt. I go first then my sister has the same thing done. We leave the building and walk through an alley to the street. We cross the street and go into another building. There we sit and wait a few minutes then we are put on a chair and get our first haircut. After we had our hair cut we took the trolly around the corner to meet up with our dad to go home. I remember my mother giving a nickel for each of us to ride the trolley.

School will start in a few weeks and we need new shoes and clothes as we may not wear the tee shirts and shorts we wear at home. We are ready for school but I am the only one who goes to school this year. My younger sister needs to wait till next year, she is not happy about the wait. We will go shopping for school clothes on the next trip into town.

The first day of school and inside the school the seats are attached to a desk. There is a black board in the front of the school behind the teachers desk. My first year in school the teacher is a man and all a first grade students learns is how to write their name, the alphabet and numbers. Once I learn to write my name I am given a book and am taught to read some simple stories. The school year goes fast for me, I am ready for the summer activities. The last day of the school year is called field day the other one room school comes to join us for a baseball game and other fun games like the three legged race.

Vacation Bible school starts right after school ends for the summer. My siblings and I attend for two weeks. Then we have a service where we show our parents what we learned.

The season for picking strawberries is started and my older sister takes my younger sister and I with her. We walk along the railroad bed to pick the wild strawberries. We had to listen for the train and stay off the tracks when the train goes by.

It didn't take us long to get way ahead of our sister on the way home. We found these big strawberries and began picking them. When my sister caught up with us she saw we were picking the berries from our Sunday school teachers garden. We had to knock on her door and tell her we were sorry for getting into her garden. When she opened her door we had to let her know we picked her strawberries. We showed Hannah the berries and told her we could pick the rest of them for her. We were allowed to keep the strawberries in our dish and she gave us a dish to pick the rest of the berries in for her. Hannah was delighted with the berries we picked and promised to bake a pie with them and we were to come and visit her the next day for a piece of the pie. This was our reward for being honest and picking the rest of her strawberries for her. She told us she is grateful for the help as she is old and has a hard time getting things done. My mom and sister made strawberry/rhubarb pie with the berries we picked. They also made homemade jam with some. My older sister was being taught how to cook and bake.

All summer after Vacation Bible school this summer I need to go to a baby sitter. I guess I will be in the way and could get hurt. One day on the way home my mother stopped in to visit my dads father, he just sits in his rocking chair in front of the spring house door. He is very thin and sick from some disease so we do not stay long today.

My dad and brothers are doing something major at home so we hurry home to help. Recently I noticed the trees and the big dirt pile are gone. I believe my father may have gotten a vacation with pay. My dad uses any unexpected money wisely on home renovations. He recently bought a furnace which he and my brothers installed during the end of the school year. I remember seeing them put up the hot air vents. The whole house will be warm in the coming winter. The parlor heater is gone, I think it is being stored somewhere. One day I ask why I have to get up so early and go with my mother and stay with an aunt every day. I don't like the babysitter cause her geese pinch me and my sister when we get out of the car. We can't even play outside cause the road is near by. We are soon taken to a different aunt she has children our age for us to play with. Every day when we go home there is much work done. I still don't know why we need a baby sitter but go along for the daily ride.

Once when we came home my dad and brother were digging in the ground and the next day the cinder blocks are delivered. On another day we come home to see that there is a big pile of lumber in the yard. There are two piles of lumber the one pile is flat on all sides. The other pile has the tree bark still on it. Every day when we arrive home from the baby sitters there is something new happening. I see a building going up and wonder what it will be.

Summer is over and my younger sister starts school too. We have a new teacher, the man has retired. The new teacher is a woman and she brings her daughter to school with her the first day. This year my mother works the evening shift in a garment shop sewing clothes. If we need help with our homework the older siblings help us and so does our dad. My dad broke his arm so he is wearing a cast and had to learn to write left handed. He is off from work while his arm heals. I have a natural tendency to be left handed. My dad helped me write my name, numbers and alphabet when I started school. Now he and my mother noticed I am writing with my left hand they are trying to get me to use my other hand to write.

I have real bad hand writing when I use my right hand. My teacher asks me why is my writing is so terrible. I explain to her what is happening at home and she decides to have a talk with my parents. She explains to my parents that my dominant hand for writing is as a left handed person. My parents decide to allow me to continue to write with my left hand finally.

I am in second grade this year and I have spelling homework. I get paired up with a girl who is left handed and her parents did not try to get her to use her right hand like my parents still try. They may have agreed with the teacher to allow me to use my dominant hand but every now and then they insist that I use my right hand. I start going to my left handed friends house to do my homework. It is hard to finish all my homework in school. I need to write each spelling word several times till I can spell the words.

My friend Karen complains to me that she needs to do some chores right away when she gets home from school and her homework before she can play. I ask her what are the chores you need to do. She tells me she needs to wash the breakfast and lunch dishes. I tell her I will help her do her chores so we can play. I tell her I have chores to do too when I get home later. When I see how many dishes she has to wash I tell her I will help you with your chores today then tomorrow you can help me with my chores. The next day when she sees the pile of dishes I have to wash she doesn't want to help. She said we will never get time to play so she went home to do her chores. The next day in school she said to me, I will never complain about my chores again now that I see how many dishes you need to do.

This year our teacher decides to take the entire 6 grades of students on regular monthly field trips. On one such hike she take us to was is called Theresa springs. It is located half way up the blue mountain. Then she tells us about the boy scout camp that was set up there. The next time she takes us on a field trip she had us hike to the top of the mountain. There she pointed out the markers pointing to the Appalachian trail that runs from Maine to the south in Georgia. She also pointed out the huge rocks on the mountain she thinks the streaks that mark the rocks are proof the ice age really did happened. She taught us about the birds common to our area, she is a member of a group of bird watchers. She showed us many different plants that were able to be eaten. Soon it will be to cold for us to take field trips with the teacher.

The teacher is a big kid herself, she brings her sled to school. There is a hill behind the one room school house where we can sleigh ride We all wait patiently for the first snow of the season. The first snow of the season turns out to be snow flurries. The second snow arrives after Thanksgiving holiday so school is closed for a week.

The township brings a big machine to move the snow drift blocking the main road. The farmer who owns the field allows us to sled down the path he uses to get to his fields. Sometimes he plants turnips in the field but most of the time he spreads manure on the field. It stinks but we tolerate the smell as we walk up the hill to ride the sleds down hill at recess and lunch time and sometimes after school.

Christmas is soon after school starts and my parents go shopping. We offer to help bring in the bags of groceries from the car we are told the rest will stay in the car trunk. The other bags are supposed to be the neighbors things she asked them to buy for her. I am told by the older siblings those things were most likely our Christmas presents.

Valentine day is coming up soon and everyone is excited to see who they will get valentines from. There are at least 30 students in the school every year.

In spring around Easter, there is a box in the kitchen with a screen on it. We sneak a peek and find brightly colored baby chicks in the box. They are to be our pets and we need to take care of their feeding and change the paper till the chicks are old enough to go out in the yard. The baby chicks grow up hopefully to be laying hens but they are roosters. Now that they are grown every time we try to go outside the roosters pick us and it hurts. They are protecting their territory. In the near future the chickens become our Sunday dinner. The school year is almost over, we can hardly wait for field day.

Spring brings a pet for us to name, this time it is a puppy. We name it Murphy, it has a shiny black and white colored fur. The white part on the dog looks like a babies bib. It needs to be trained to ask to go out to do its eliminating or I need to clean the mess it makes. Small children waste food and left overs from meals are used to feed the dog. The dog is fully grown and it gets out of the yard. By fall there are puppies to give away, boy dogs do not have babies so it must have been a female dog.

School is out for the Summer again and first we go to Vacation Bible school for two weeks. Then after that we go to our aunt's home. What ever the men are doing we will be in the way. Every day we come home we see changes, the garden is bigger this year.

It is almost time for school to start again and we go shopping for school clothes. We go for another ride in the car for clothes and shoe shopping. This time there is no trolley to ride. The store we shop in is not a large department store the owner sells shoes and clothes. We walk along the main street for all the things we need then walk back to the car to go home.

Meals have to be made and all the things bought for school must be put away.

This year when school starts I will be in third grade, my uncle and aunt stop in for a visit. She will be going along with my mother to work in a garment manufacturing company. My homework is much harder but I continue to be an A student. I am a natural in spelling class, the teacher gives us new words to learn the meanings and use them in sentences. I learn to spell the words quickly and do not need to write them over and over like the rest of the class. This year we are trying to get someone entered into the national spelling bee. My teacher hopes that I will be the person entering the contest.

When the teacher does try outs for the national spelling bee she divides the entire group of students in half. Some stand along one wall the rest stand at the other wall. Each side is given a word to spell. If they spell it correctly they stay standing, if they spell it wrong they need to sit down at their desk. This game makes spelling fun for all the students.

We also have an uncle who visits us on a regular basis in the evening. He is a music teacher he taught my older siblings to play some instruments. Then before going home again he would sing his silly songs to entertain us. He could play the piano, guitar, violin and many other instruments. We had a baby grand piano in our living room for many years.

I am entering the fourth grade this year and so far I have had perfect attendance in elementary school. The first day of school is spent with the teacher handing out pencils and tablets. She tells us that she has arranged for the entire group to go on a nice field trip later in the year. We try our best to get her to reveal her surprise with no luck. I think the year will be almost the same as any other year just a little harder. This year the first grade class is the biggest ever, there are 10 in the class.

This year the farmer has turnips planted in the field around the school. Our teacher uses every opportunity to turn something into a lesson. She explains that the farmer will feed the turnips to his dairy cows. She did her research and discovered that the turnips the cows eat will help them get through the winter months when they will eat mostly dried grain and alfalfa. The turnips may enhance the milk production. I think it may be the butter fat is richer.

I think figured out where the teacher planned to take us on our field trip. I waited till the school day ended and asked her if she was taking us on a tour through a farmers day! She allowed me to think I guessed the field trip and told me not to tell anyone. It was to remain a big secret till all the arrangements were set and all permission slips were signed.

Finally the wait is over, we will take a bus to the local dairy to learn how milk is treated, then bottled as whole milk, butter milk and skim milk. and made into products like butter and cheese.

The new school year I will be in the sixth grade. I am loving the education part of my life, my grades are good so the teacher allows me to be a coach for some who have a hard time learning to spell the word lists she gives out. I am being prepared for the next level of my education in Junior High School. I will have a guided tour of the high school by going along with a former sixth grade student who is now in seventh grade.

www.ingramcontent.com/pod-product-compliance
Lightning Source LLC
Chambersburg PA
CBHW051604120626
46551CB00013B/1668